Baby Chicken or Baby Duck?

by Christina Leaf

BELLWETHER MEDIA • MINNEAPOLIS, MN

Blastoff! Readers are carefully developed by literacy experts to build reading stamina and move students toward fluency by combining standards-based content with developmentally appropriate text.

Level 1 provides the most support through repetition of high-frequency words, light text, predictable sentence patterns, and strong visual support.

Level 2 offers early readers a bit more challenge through varied sentences, increased text load, and text-supportive special features.

Level 3 advances early-fluent readers toward fluency through increased text load, less reliance on photos, advancing concepts, longer sentences, and more complex special features.

★ **Blastoff! Universe**

This edition first published in 2025 by Bellwether Media, Inc.

No part of this publication may be reproduced in whole or in part without written permission of the publisher. For information regarding permission, write to Bellwether Media, Inc., Attention: Permissions Department, 6012 Blue Circle Drive, Minnetonka, MN 55343.

Library of Congress Cataloging-in-Publication Data

Names: Leaf, Christina, author.
Title: Baby chicken or baby duck? / by Christina Leaf.
Description: Minneapolis, MN : Bellwether Media, Inc., 2025. | Series: Blastoff! readers: who is cuter? | Includes bibliographical references and index. | Audience: Ages 5-8 | Audience: Grades K-1 | Summary: "Developed by literacy experts for students in kindergarten through grade three, this book introduces the differences between baby chickens and baby ducks to young readers through leveled text and related photos"– Provided by publisher.
Identifiers: LCCN 2024003091 (print) | LCCN 2024003092 (ebook) | ISBN 9798886870299 (library binding) | ISBN 9798893041439 (paperback) | ISBN 9781644878736 (ebook)
Subjects: LCSH: Chicks–Juvenile literature. | Ducklings–Juvenile literature.
Classification: LCC SF487.5 .L425 2025 (print) | LCC SF487.5 (ebook) | DDC 636.5/07–dc23/eng/20240304
LC record available at https://lccn.loc.gov/2024003091
LC ebook record available at https://lccn.loc.gov/2024003092

Text copyright © 2025 by Bellwether Media, Inc. BLASTOFF! READERS and associated logos are trademarks and/or registered trademarks of Bellwether Media, Inc. Bellwether Media is a division of Chrysalis Education Group.

Editor: Suzane Nguyen   Designer: Andrea Schneider

Printed in the United States of America, North Mankato, MN.

Table of Contents

Chicks and Ducklings!	4
Beaks and Bills	8
Land and Water	12
Who Is Cuter?	20
Glossary	22
To Learn More	23
Index	24

Chicks and Ducklings!

Baby chickens are called chicks. Baby ducks are ducklings.

These birds **hatch** from eggs. Both have soft feathers. They are so fluffy!

Beaks and Bills

Chicks have pointy **beaks**. They eat seeds. Ducklings have rounded **bills**. They eat plants.

bill

beak

Chicks have pointed toes. They dig for food. Ducklings have **webbed feet** to swim.

webbed feet

pointed toes

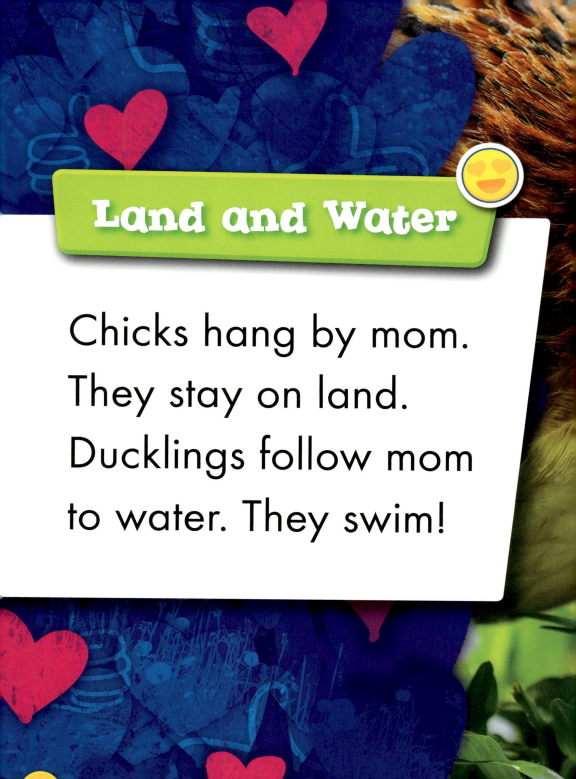

Land and Water

Chicks hang by mom. They stay on land. Ducklings follow mom to water. They swim!

Chicks **peck** the ground for food. Ducklings find food in water.

pecking for food

Most older chicks live in **coops**. Some ducklings live in coops. Others live in the wild.

coop

Chicks say peep.
Ducklings say quack.
Which baby is cuter?

Who Is Cuter?

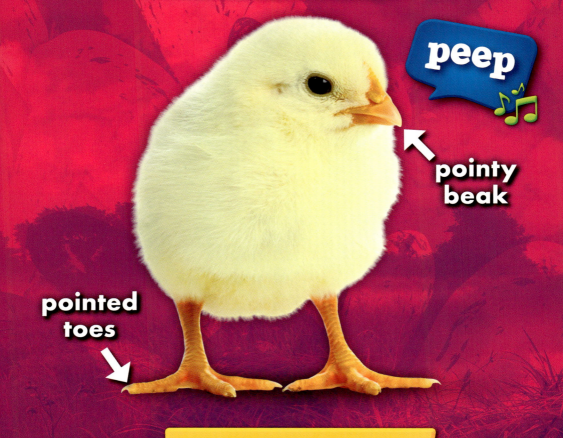

peep

pointy beak

pointed toes

Baby Chicken

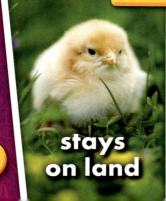
stays on land

pecks for food

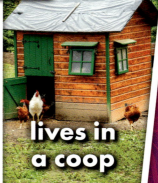
lives in a coop

Glossary

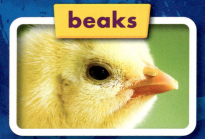
beaks
the mouths of chickens

hatch
to break out of an egg

bills
the mouths of ducks

peck
to pick at and eat bits of food with a beak

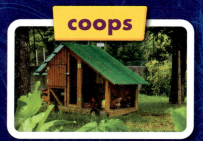
coops
homes for chickens and some ducks

webbed feet
feet with thin skin between the toes

To Learn More

AT THE LIBRARY

Anderhagen, Anna. *Ducklings: A First Look*. Minneapolis, Minn.: Lerner Publications, 2025.

Neuenfeldt, Elizabeth. *Baby Chickens*. Minneapolis, Minn.: Bellwether Media, 2023.

Rathburn, Betsy. *Baby Ducks*. Minneapolis, Minn.: Bellwether Media, 2022.

ON THE WEB

FACTSURFER

Factsurfer.com gives you a safe, fun way to find more information.

1. Go to www.factsurfer.com.

2. Enter "baby chicken or baby duck" into the search box and click 🔍.

3. Select your book cover to see a list of related content.

Index

chickens, 4
coops, 16, 17
beaks, 8, 9
bills, 8, 9
birds, 6
dig, 10
ducks, 4
eggs, 6
feathers, 6, 7
food, 10, 14, 15
hatch, 6, 7
land, 12
mom, 12, 13
peck, 14, 15
peep, 18, 19
plants, 8

pointed toes, 10, 11
quack, 18, 19
seeds, 8
swim, 10, 12
water, 12, 14
webbed feet, 10, 11
wild, 16

The images in this book are reproduced through the courtesy of: Perky Pets / Alamy Stock Photos/ Alamy, front cover (chick); Natalia Vasylkivska, front cover (duckling), p. 20 (stays on land); Valentina Razumova, Valentina Rasumova | Dreamstime.com, pp. 3 (chick), 4-5, 6-7; Tsekhmister, pp. 3 (duckling), 21 (duckling); thieury, p. 5; Malgorzata Surawska p. 7; Uros Poteko / Alamy Stock Photo/ Ton Bangkeaw pp. 8-9; Alamy, p. 9; forstbreath, pp. 10-11; Anneka, p. 11; HunsaBKK, pp. 12-13; mono2mono/ Adobe Stock, p. 13; Star Moroz, pp. 14-15; Volodymyr Maksymchuk, pp. 15, 16-17; Andi Edwards, p. 17; Angela Forker | Dreamstime.com, pp. 18-19; anca enache/ Adobe Stock, p. 19; matooker/ Getty Images, p. 20 (chick); Nataliia Maksymenko, p. 20 (pecks for food); ENRIQUE ALAEZ PEREZ, p. 20 (lives in coops); Enjoylife2, p. 21 (swims); Matias Gauthier, p. 21 (finds food in water); Evgenia Rotanova, p. 21 (lives in coops or the wild); Santirat/ Adobe Stock, p. 22 (beaks); Naypong Studio, p. 22 (bills); Peter Klampfer, p. 22 (coops); Arpad Nagy-Bagoly/ Adobe Stock, p. 22 (hatch); MilousSK p. 22 (peck); Matthew Williams-Ellis p. 22 (webbed feet).